The Rapid Advance Process
for Attracting Loving Relationships

**Ellie Izzo, PhD and
Vicki Carpel Miller, BSN, MS, LMFT**

Just Stop Picking Losers!

Published by:
HCI Press
7701 E. Indian School Rd. Ste. F
Scottsdale, AZ 85251 USA
www.hcipress.com

A Note to the Reader: The information, ideas and suggestions in this book are not intended as a substitute for professional advice. Before following any suggestions contained in this book you should consult your personal physician or mental health professional. Neither the authors nor the publisher shall be liable or responsible for any loss or damage allegedly arising as a consequence of your use or application of any information or suggestions in this book.

Library of Congress Control Number: 2011939248

ISBN-10: 1-936268-24-8
ISBN-13: 978-1-936268-24-5

High Conflict Institute Press
Scottsdale, Arizona

Book Design by www.KarrieRoss.com
Images from istockphoto.com

ALSO BY ELLIE IZZO AND VICKI CARPEL MILLER

Second-Hand Shock: Surviving & Overcoming Vicarious Trauma
Just Stop Doing That!
Just Stop Eating That!

ALSO BY ELLIE IZZO

The Bridge To I Am

INTRODUCTION

Why is it that when you meet the "right person," you seem to know it's "right" in a minute? But when you meet the "wrong person," you don't realize it's "wrong" for at least a couple of years? We heard this joke on late night television and while we found it to be very amusing, we also saw a lot of truth in it. How many of you have remained in bad relationships with a "loser," or more clinically, a maladjusted person, long after you knew being with that person was no longer helpful to your emotional health?

Everyone wants love in their life. It seems to give purpose and meaning to just about everything we do. But some people's idea of love can literally kill. You've probably heard the startling statistics that the number one person of interest in homicide investigations is the victim's significant other. Talk about being with the wrong person!

Why is it acceptable for many people to remain in relationships with abusers, misfits, deadbeats and losers?

It's an issue for you. You want to know. That's why you bought this book. Rest assured, you are not alone.

Everyone wants love in their life.

We want you to have love in your life, but healthy love. The kind of love that helps you grow, brings out the best in you, and creates a lot of positive energy. Something is blocking your ability to attract that kind of love. This book will help you remove the obstacles to magnetizing a wonderful love in your direction and most of all help you to **Just Stop Picking Losers**!

CONTENTS

Part One:

Part Two:
The Rapid Advance Workbook

PART ONE

CHAPTER ONE

Picking Losers Isn't Your Problem, It's Your Distraction

You don't start out in a new relationship looking to pick a loser. Who would do that? What often happens first is that thing called chemistry. You meet someone and your pheromones go crazy. You feel the erotic heat between you and you think *this person is everything you've been looking for. But what are you really looking for at that point?* Is it love, or is it kissing, touching, skin contact, sex? Maybe you're looking for a space-filler; a warm body just so you don't have to be alone. One lady shared with us her "telling" experience upon getting divorced. This experience occurred during the first week after her husband moved out. Late one evening her friend called to find out how she was doing. Her friend asked, "So how does it feel to have no one in the bed?" She paused, felt her blood boil, and asserted, "Excuse me! **I'M** in the bed. That's somebody!"

Many people believe that they have a missing part if they aren't in a relationship; they feel incomplete. They, in truth, see themselves at a loss. At some level, maybe subconsciously, they believe **they** are a loser. They think latching onto someone else will remedy that loss. But it doesn't. We believe that getting coupled is **not** a cure for being single. The state of being single is **not** a disease. Being coupled and being single are two mutually exclusive ways to be. Each has its advantages and each has its challenges. One is not necessarily better or worse than the other.

> *You don't start out in a new relationship looking to pick a loser.*

The problem with people who think they are not whole unless they are in a relationship is that they seek out someone, anyone, to fill that loss or void. The irony is that filling that void is strictly an inside job. We call this a case of the "tail wagging the dog." These people believe, "If I get someone in my life, then I'll be whole." Wrong! The appropriate statement goes, "When I become whole, then I'll get someone in my life."

Those of you who have a case of the tail wagging the dog attract the wrong type of people into your life because you are looking for someone to fill an empty space; one which only you can fill. If you are in a room with one hundred people, and ninety-nine are whole, you will attract the one who isn't whole until you achieve that completeness for yourself.

Sorry, we don't mean to be harsh, but when you look to someone else to complete you, you will attract someone who is incomplete and then the games begin! They may not begin right away, but rest assured they will begin.

Red Flags for Spotting Losers

- Drinks too much
- Drug addiction
- Can't hold down a job
- Has poor family relationships
- Has been in trouble with the law
- Doesn't pay child support or spousal maintenance from prior marriage
- Doesn't follow through with agreements
- Lies
- Opportunist
- Has entitlement issues
- Verbally and/or physically abusive
- Promiscuous
- Gambling addiction
- Pornography addiction
- Internet addiction

- Asks you for money
- Wants to move in with you right away
- Doesn't take "no" for an answer

There will be some immediate red flags, but you'll ignore them because you think you are now complete. Pity, because when you are with someone who is incomplete, you then leave yourself and try to fill their incompleteness instead of your own perceived void. You mistakenly believe that if you fix them, they'll never leave you. The paradox here is that **you** have left you, and that self abandonment grows deeper and deeper while you put all your effort into someone else. This never works out well.

When you're with a loser you start to carry their feelings and you sacrifice your own.

After a while you forget your own mind: your own thoughts, desires, needs and boundaries. You are so caught up in the other person that you have lost yourself. We often say to clients, "If we need to take your partner's temperature, all we have to do is put our hand on your forehead!" You do this because you don't believe you have enough merit; that just being yourself isn't enough to sustain the relationship. When you're with a loser you start to carry their feelings and you sacrifice your own. This is part of the insanity. Some people will go to extraordinary lengths and endure immeasurable amounts of pain just to avoid being alone. Why is that? What comes up for you when you are alone? We think it is fear. We think it is fear because if you don't think you are complete, then you can never be alone. The faulty thought pattern repeats in your brain that if you are incomplete and then left alone, you will die. We don't want to get all heady and morose on you right now, but when you attract a loser who becomes your full-time job, takes up all your time and attention and drains you of your spiritual energy, you remain distracted from your fear of being alone. Imagine if you faced that fear, looked at it square in the eye, and conquered it. Can you picture the type of person you would attract when you are no longer afraid to stand on your own?

The faulty thought pattern repeats in your brain that if you are incomplete and then left alone, you will die.

We believe that people who see themselves as incomplete and afraid to be alone are in a state of disconnect from their higher mind. It is only through a strong neural connection to the higher mind that you are able to access intangible traits such as courage, faith and trust in yourself; believing you are complete and can stand on your own two feet. This "disconnect" from your higher mind or spiritual self happened outside of your awareness and at an earlier time in your life. Come with us through the **Rapid Advance Process,** which will take you through 5 steps for reconnecting with the most powerful part of your identity. We call these steps The 5 **R**'s:

- Revealing Your History
- Recognizing Your Impasse
- Releasing Your Past
- Responding To Fear
- Reconnecting To Your Spirit

When you have completed the steps, you will have everything you need to see yourself as whole and complete. Then you can attract amazing love into your life, and you will **Stop Picking Losers!**

CHAPTER TWO

Please Recover From Having a Mother, or Revealing Your History

You didn't come into this world seeing yourself as incomplete or feeling afraid. You were born a little ball of love; you were precious and innocent until life started happening to you. Your "incomplete self," or ego, began developing as a defense against feeling afraid. That's just the way it is. This happens to everyone. You may think that your personal childhood history holds no triggers or truly upsetting events, but in reality your childhood holds the key to how you have come to see yourself as disconnected and not whole. Many of us have forgotten much of the past, or perhaps have developed a selective recall about it. We are not suggesting that you get bogged down in your past, but reviewing it has its advantages. This review provides an opportunity to use your history as a catalyst to make positive changes in the here and now.

We are interested in how your judgment or perception of some of your historical events may have caused this "disconnect," or as we call it, an "Impasse," to your spiritual self. This Impasse prevents you from bridging to, or accessing, the higher part of your brain that houses the qualities of courage, strength, forgiveness, faith, trust and hope. These qualities are necessary for you to feel complete. You then have no need to look for someone else to fill any void. You have it all!

When the pathway to your spiritual self is blocked...you cannot access your higher mind, and you become stuck neurologically in lower brain thinking.

When the pathway to your spiritual self is blocked, or develops an Impasse, you cannot access your higher mind, and you become stuck neurologically in lower brain thinking. This thinking is based on instincts of fight, flight or freeze, and is driven by fear. You feel separated and alone. This is really scary and becomes the flawed underlying motivation to seek another person out rather than to rely on your own internal resources. Take one cup of your history; add to it 2 tablespoons of how you attached as a child; add a quarter cup of your subconscious memory; add a pinch of your parents' traits or characteristics, and you've got a foolproof recipe for whether or not you will choose a loser.

Sigmund Freud was known for saying that your mother or your father is your first lover. Don't get freaked out by this remark. He didn't necessarily mean it in terms of the taboo of incest. He meant it in terms of the unconscious parental memories that get triggered by people to whom you feel attracted. When you follow through on the attraction, you then unconsciously attribute to the other person the qualities you experienced in one or both of your parents. It could be a tiny nuance between the two of you that triggers a flood of parental issues that color your perception of the person you are with. It doesn't have to be something intense and dramatic. It also doesn't have to be something bad.

Whistling Willie

Emma and Willie had only been married a short time. They had a whirlwind courtship of about three months. In fact, after their second date, Emma had a clear feeling that Willie was "the one." Four months later, they were married. Setting up house together was a very enjoyable time in their relationship. They were in the stage of establishing their roles, and even though Emma worked a full time job as a teacher, she would arrive home before Willie and prepare a meal. As she set the table, she would keep an ear open for the garage door being raised - her signal that Willie was home.

One night Emma was at the other end of the house when Willie arrived. She stopped in her tracks when she suddenly heard someone robustly whistling from the garage area. For a second, it made her head spin. Willie was whistling exactly the same melodic tune her father had whistled every evening upon returning home from his long day's work! Her father had been dead for two years. Willie's whistle triggered a lot of body memories for Emma. She felt like a little girl for a moment and experienced the strong feelings of affection she had always carried for her father. When she went to greet Willie, she was especially affectionate. Willie remarked, "Wow! What's up?" She responded, "Oh, nothing, I just love you so!"

A couple of months later, Emma's mother was visiting at dinner time. They were sitting at the kitchen table together when Willie entered the house. As usual, he let out that whistle to let Emma know that he was home. Emma's mother shot her a shocked look of surprise. Emma said, "I know, Mom, it sounds just like Dad." Twenty years later, Emma and Willie are still happily married. Emma still melts when Willie comes through the door, whistling his arrival to his bride.

That's the good news about historical influences on who you find yourself attracted to. Unfortunately, we have to address the bad news. As much as there could be positive triggers from your partner, there are also negative nuances and attributes that trigger sinister memories within you of one or both of your parents.

*...the parent you feel the least loved
by is the one you search for in your
primary relationship.*

Every child wants their parents' love and regard. Sadly, there are many children who don't get it, but every child wants it. When a child comes into the world, the child needs and looks for a positive loving attachment with its parents. Many children get this love; others don't. Children who have unfinished "attachment" business with a parent carry memories of longing into adulthood. When they are looking for a partner, those longings become like magnets and grown children will actually find themselves attracted to people who possess certain attributes of their parents. Unconsciously, the grown child is attracted to this person in part because they offer another opportunity to finish the unfinished parental business of receiving unconditional love and acceptance.

What if your parent had problems? An emotional disturbance, addiction, was an abuser, a misfit, or a loser? Guess who you're at risk to be looking for? Furthermore, the parent you feel the least loved by is the one you search for in your primary relationship. Revealing your history is absolutely paramount in examining the types of people you attract because your early attachments, or lack thereof, set the stage for who you seek out as an adult.

Manipulative Michael and Rigid Rena

Michael and Rena had been living together for two years. Michael was a mortgage broker and Rena was a successful, high-profile cosmetic surgeon. They described themselves as having a huge chemistry from the moment they met. Michael went to see Rena professionally to have a mole removed from his cheek. They got to talking, and soon were meeting for a drink at happy hour. Two months later, they moved in together. Rena thought Michael was adorable. She described him as a little teddy bear; soft and huggable. He was a breath of fresh air to her. Rena had had her lion's share of successful, arrogant guys. Michael was down-to-earth, soft-spoken, and let her run the show. Michael loved Rena's strength and organizational skills. He thought of her as his hero; capable, strong and responsible, but sometimes demanding. In the beginning, Michael had great respect for Rena's attributes and she for his, but when the love-dust settled, all the attribute blessings turned into the relationship burdens.

During our first meeting with Rena and Michael, Rena was invested in criticizing Michael. We stopped her and asked her to consider why she thought she was so triggered? Sure enough, when she revealed her history, a lot of light was shed on how their relationship had quickly evolved into a re-creation of their families of origin.

Rena had grown up in a family where her father was a successful cardiothoracic surgeon. He was rarely home, treated her mother with icy distance, and perceived himself as superior. Her father and mother had met at the hospital where he was doing his residency and she was an x-ray tech. Once they had children, her mother remained at home and never returned to the workforce, but that did not matter to her father; he still treated her mother like one of his staff.

Michael's father had been a Major in the Army, and their family moved numerous times to accommodate his career. He was very controlling of the family finances and only doled out money to Michael's mother in very small amounts. Michael had shared with Rena memories of his mother sneaking money from his father's wallet in order to buy herself some of the extras that her husband would deny her. When his father's car pulled into the garage, everyone would stand at attention and then dash for their rooms. Rena said Michael knew that when his father was home, his mother's time would be occupied so he would need to fend for himself. Michael's mother was passive and submissive to the father's every need when he was at home. Michael was very close with his mother, Rena said, and never had much of a relationship with his father. Michael longed for father-son time together, which never happened, as his father died of cancer shortly after Michael and Rena moved in together.

When Rena became more aware of the impact both her history and Michael's had on their relationship, she was able to get out of the critical mode and pay more attention to her own behaviors, rather than focusing on Michael's. Her ongoing rage at Michael was breaking his spirit, and Rena was feeling awful about herself because of her bad behavior. Instead of trying to change Michael

*and become enraged when he did not change, her focus
turned to whether or not she wanted to remain committed to Michael in the marriage.*

Historically, when a parent ignores or neglects, or is
unkind, verbally abusive, or physically violent toward
a child, the greatest damage is done to the child on
a spiritual level and that child then begins to operate from
fear. As a result, the neural pathways to that child's
higher mind begin to atrophy and the child becomes less
and less able to connect with the higher mind – that part
of thinking that gives him or her courage, trust and faith
in him/herself.

Take out a notebook or journal and write your
personal history as if it were a narrative or story.
Take your time. Pay attention and don't leave stuff out.
It is important to allow yourself to reveal your history.
It holds the blueprint of who you are attracted to, and it
holds the key to how you can magnetize wonderfully
intimate and fulfilling love.

CHAPTER THREE

Round and Round, or
Recognizing the Impasse

Now that you have revealed your history, you are ready to recognize your Impasse–that place in your experience where an early fear becomes triggered in the here and now. When you are triggered, you become fearful. In order to avoid the fearful feeling, you distract yourself by focusing on, and trying to fix, your partner's problems. This becomes a circular experience because each and every time you try to fix your partner's problems, you have actually denied them an opportunity to step up to the plate, take responsibility, and remedy their personal life issues. So the irony here is that you are actually reinforcing the very problem you mistakenly think you are fixing. Round and round you go. These patterns become so addictive that even if you break away from them, you will be seduced, tempted and eventually relapse—unless you recognize your Impasse. You've heard the line people often ask about battered spouses, "Why do they always go back?" Well now you have the answer.

Common Traits of People Who Pick Losers

- People-pleaser
- Unwilling to speak up
- Overly compliant
- Not in touch with your own needs
- Conflict-avoidant
- Giving 'til it hurts
- Isolated
- Brainwashed
- Having sex for the wrong reasons
- Scared of the other's reaction
- Low self-esteem
- Lack of confidence
- Challenged in general communication skill
- Manipulative
- Covert

You are triggered in the present because the current trigger is in some way related to a past event that caused you to feel afraid, and broke your spirit. Just like a small child, you perceive that you have no internal resources to overcome the fear, and so you distract yourself by working on somebody else's problems. As long as you are outside of your own body, you don't have to feel afraid. These distractions are no longer helpful if you want to **Stop Picking Losers**.

Common Impasses that make you feel afraid:

- Abandonment
- Being hurt
- Inferiority, or not being good enough
- Commitment
- Not being lovable
- Loss of competence
- Failure
- Success
- The unknown
- Losing control
- Death
- Divorce
- and numerous others

Marrying Martin

Martin loved being married. He thought it was the only way to be. He was a successful architect who worked for years to create an internationally acclaimed firm. He was well-known in the community, and everyone loved him. He had worked for years on his own personal growth...or so he thought.

Martin met a lovely girl who had a severe emotional disorder, but he didn't seem to notice it at the time. He thought she was just high strung.

Several months into the marriage he began to experience panic attacks. In order for him to distract himself from the reality of his wife and his life, he began traveling for work much of the time. This, of course, only exacerbated her psychological symptoms of dependence and histrionics.

By the time he came to us for counseling, Martin was haggard, thin, and very depressed. It took months for him to muster up the courage to leave this toxic relationship. The divorce was drawn out and his wife never understood why he divorced her, and what made him so unhappy.

He finally wrote a very large check to end the divorce debacle. He began to move on. We bet you think this story is over...but it's not.

Martin became one of the most sought-after bachelors in his town. He told us that he would never marry someone with a mental disorder again. He even went so far as to state that he wanted us to meet with his next fiancée so that he could be sure he was not making the same mistake twice. He never followed his own well-thought-out advice.

He came back to us some months later to tell us he was engaged. At first we were delighted to hear of his *good fortune and wanted to know all about her. He told us she was very competent, extremely well-organized, neat as a pin, and very thoughtful. She was an extremely beautiful divorcée with two young boys. The boys loved him and he loved the idea of a ready-made family.*

Martin did mention that she lacked spontaneity, but he sloughed it off by stating, "Well, you can't have everything." We focused on it by stating, "It sounds to us like she may have some challenges around anxiety. How will that fit with your desire to pick up and go on the spur of the moment?" He remarked that it wasn't that important to him. Needless to say, not more than two months after he married her, he was back in our office, wanting to know why he keeps picking disturbed women!

When he revealed his history, Martin spoke of a physically and verbally abusive father, a removed and distant mother, and tremendous fear of what might happen if something set his father off. He observed his older sister's beatings and his mother's apparent indifference and escape through her social activities. Martin recognized his Impasse as fear of abandonment through neglect, and his attraction to women who were unavailable was the magnet of his childhood longing for a caring, protective mom. In his need to fix what he never got from his mother, he kept finding himself attracted to personality types just like her.

Your Impasse is the key to understanding why you continue to pick losers. Not surprisingly, all Impasses have their root in some perceived abandonment. Remember, history repeats itself. If you have unresolved fears from the past, you are at risk to have these fears come up again and again with other people. These fears rear their ugly heads when our partner engages in a behavior that triggers a painful memory. This happens outside of your awareness, and you end up repeatedly trying to create a happy historical ending with a modern-day partner.

> *If you have unresolved fears from the past, you are at risk to have these fears come up again and again with other people.*

This wouldn't be so bad if you picked someone with whom you can authentically open your heart about your past. This person would then support you and work on this with you in the spirit of helping you to heal. But losers can't do that, because they are in their own world of hurt—one that they themselves are clueless about. They are busy re-enacting their own childhood pain with you. We call this the Toxic Tango. It is an exhausting dance with no end.

Lisa and Bryan in the Toxic Tango

Lisa and Bryan met at a college fraternity party and immediately hit it off. They began dating, and shortly thereafter Lisa had a complaint. Bryan was always 30 minutes late. Even when they had a specific time to be somewhere, he was late. This drove Lisa mad. Lisa had a mission; to get Bryan to show up on time. In order to manage him, she came up with some clever tricks. For instance, she would tell him that they needed to be at an event one hour earlier than the actual time, hoping that he would arrive in time to get them there without being late. Sometimes, she used the repetitive telephoning angle, calling him with the same question, "Have you left yet?" His response was always the sam, "In a few minutes." Other tricks she used were screaming, begging, cajoling and threatening; none of which were effective. Not only were they always late but Lisa was continuously a wreck. Bryan, on the other hand, was as calm, cool and collected as ever. Lisa eventually became exhausted in this Toxic Tango and came to see us.

Lisa revealed her history, which included a passive father who was directed by an intrusive, dominating wife. Lisa's father would make many agreements with her, and then either forget about them or unilaterally decide that they weren't important enough for follow-through. Lisa shared her sadness and disappointment about her father's behavior. The fear she carried—her Impasse—was that in some way, she must have not been a lovable enough daughter for her father to take seriously, and follow through on his commitments to her. The challenge was that not only did Lisa take Bryan's tardiness personally, she took it "historically," and so her reaction was exaggerated given the nature of his transgression. Unfortunately, her reaction didn't fix Bryan's chronic lateness; in fact, it made it worse. The more she carried on, the later he'd run.

Once you recognize the Impasse as you set it up in the present, you might notice that you move around in a chronic state of separation anxiety. Separation anxiety refers to the upset a child feels when he or she must detach from a parent. Consider this thought: what if separation anxiety is actually the chronic underlying distress you feel as a result of being separated from the most loving and nurturing spiritual part of YOURSELF? If this is true, we remain separated by fear in adulthood and latch onto losers. We then try to fix them as a way to avoid feeling this unpleasant anxiety. Imagine what might happen if you were to recognize and then meet this anxiety head-on. Then, maybe your relationship choices would look very different.

Billy The Bully

Billy came to see us after his third wife threatened to leave him unless he got counseling. Billy had been involved in two failed marriages due to his incessant habit of bullying the women he was with. The women he would attract brought nothing to the table; they were lazy, they refused to work, they were "gold-diggers," and they abused alcohol and recreational drugs. They were very high maintenance, but they put up with Billy's bullying. He constantly felt taken advantage of, taken for granted, and resentful. Billy would tell these women to clean his place and to make him dinner. He would call them names, and threaten to take away their cars and their charge cards if they didn't comply with his requests. He was clearly unhappy with the type of women he chose, but all the bullying in the world wasn't going to change the nature of these women.

Billy revealed his history, and while he had positive enough parents, he was teased and made fun of in elementary school. He had very poor vision and wore very thick glasses. He had buck teeth, and the other children called him Bucky Beaver. He went home and asked his parents for help, but they refused to get involved. They told him to ignore the other kids, but the taunting never stopped. By the time Billy finished middle school, he had hardened his heart and was invested in turning the tables. He was so unpopular that he hardly dated at all throughout high school, and people grew to fear him because of his caustic attitude and nastiness. When Billy told us his experiences in elementary school he started to sob, and shared how scared he was to go to school every day, and how scared he was to be made fun of by the other kids. It turns out that behind the bullying façade, there was a very anxious little boy. The childhood taunting broke Billy's spirit. He lost his innocence, and his behavior made him look like he was full of the devil. Billy realized that his Impasse was rooted in spiritual separation anxiety.

Some "Loser" Personality Traits

Self-centered	Lacking compassion
Substance-abusive	Non-committal
Brainwashing	Gold digging
Inflexible	No spiritual life
Erratic Behaviors	Trouble with the law
Demeaning	Begrudging
Blaming	Dishonest
Chronically unhappy	Cheating
Verbally abusive	Never remorseful
Flat personality	Avoidant
Dismissive	Lazy
Selfish	Reactive
Condescending	Anxiety-ridden
Cheap	Very negative
Sexually controlling	Violent

Look at the underlying and silent themes from your family of origin to help you recognize your Impasse. Many times these themes appear subtle and unimportant from a grown-up point of view. For example, in some families boys are treated differently than girls. In other families, some religious practices crowd out healthy and direct communication. Money issues, changing values, and family secrets can all contribute to creating Impasses. In other situations, how others saw the family might have been more important than what was truly happening within it. In recognizing your Impasse, don't always look for the obvious. Many times it is the unspoken themes or codes of silence that can drive the Impasse forward, sometimes for generations.

When a child doesn't get the unconditional acceptance they need from either parent, a part of them never really quite matures and individuates. They look grown up, and in a lot of ways they act grown up. But somewhere in their subconscious is a frightened little child who craves this love. This little child can pop up at any time, just like a jack-in-the box, trying to complete this perceived missing part of their development. It most frequently happens in primary love relationships. The challenge is to notice that it is happening early on in a relationship, rather than coming to realize it after it is too late.

The challenge is to notice that it is happening early on in a relationship, rather than coming to realize it after it is too late.

Attachment to the past through fear has an addictive quality to it. The familiarity of being stuck at the Impasse has a perverse sense of comfort, simply because you are so used to being fearful and anxious. You remain attached to the associated separation anxiety we spoke of earlier—comfortably uncomfortable is one way to think of this. By recognizing in the present that you are replaying an updated version of a scary historical scene from the past, you can then experience, rather than avoid, the separation anxiety that gets triggered in the replay. If you can do this, you are at the gateway of stopping your need to fix somebody else (the parental symbol) so you can be better.

Recognizing your Impasse is your wake-up call to experience your separation from your loving self or spirit. When you begin the journey of reconnecting to your higher mind, you will know that you are not abandoned, and are therefore never really alone.

CHAPTER FOUR

It's Old News,
or Releasing the Past

When we remain attached to the past, we cannot connect to our innocent spiritual self or higher mind. This spiritual self helps us stay peacefully centered in the here and now. Having recognized your personal Impasse, and having made the decision to no longer retreat from it through taking on someone else's hopeless causes, you can now begin to access your higher mind or spiritual self.

In the beginning this might be experienced as a challenge, because you are in the throes of separation anxiety as you call upon yourself to "Stop Picking Losers!"

However, what is different now is that you can take a leap of faith—that in stopping this distraction, you can find your way back to your spirit, that part of you that was broken at an earlier point in your life. As we give fear over to our spiritual mind, we receive spiritual traits in ourselves such as courage, trust, honesty, forgiveness and faith.

Take a moment to define the past. It is commonly thought of as "the time before or time gone by." What does that mean? The past is a span of time. Is that tangible? We don't think so. Your memories of time gone by are all that really exist now, and they exist only in your mind. Memories are not really the past; they are only perceptions of it. Have you ever experienced an event with another person where you were present for the same period of time in that shared situation, and later, you both recalled the incident differently? It is important to realize that *what* you remember has far less impact than *how* you remember. The historical action is over. It is only your judgment of it that actually remains.

A parent's memory of family life may be very different from their child's. The parents may remember the family situation to have been wonderful with their roles as very involved, positive and caring. The child's perception may be infinitely different. The child may remember the relationship with the parents to have been, at times, unsafe. Perhaps when the parents were angry, under the influence, or absent either through physical or mental illness, they were perceived by the child as abandoning. This is very frightening to a child, because after all, an abandoned child will die. Perhaps these parents were preoccupied with their own lives and the child began to feel abandoned and unloved. Young children do not yet have the cognitive ability or the brain development to rationalize that a parent's unavailability is about the parent and has nothing to do with the child's value. A child of any age thinks the parent's unavailability or abandonment is not because of the parent, but because the child himself is not lovable enough. Now, we ask you, who was right in their perception, and who was wrong? Neither? Both?

Memories are not really the past;
they are only perceptions of it.

When this child decides to release the past, he or she understands that the existing memory of the parent's behavior was simply one point of view. When this same child overcomes or rises above his fear of those upsetting or scary situations, he also relinquishes *his personal judgment* about his lovability in the eyes of those scary parents. The point is that a perception of your past exists in your mind and that is all there is left of it. The events themselves are much less meaningful than how you took in the events as they occurred. How you took them in, experienced them, processed them, and judged yourself in the context of them, is what makes up your perception of them.

Parental Penelope and Andrew-with-an-Attitude

Penelope was the firstborn daughter in an alcoholic

family. Both of her parents had managed habits, and begin drinking nightly at the designated cocktail hour around five o'clock. Once they started drinking, they couldn't stop. Sometimes there were other couples at the house, sometimes they were alone. The predictable scene included the parents drinking on the patio while the children ran in and out, whining for them to come in: "Mommy, pleeeeeeease. Come in, I'm hungry." And there followed the classic dishonest response, "Just another minute......I'm coming in." But they never came in. Penelope, by default, became the stand-in parent, taking care of her three younger siblings. There was homework to do, bath time, not to mention the preparation of dinner. The parents were never overtly mean. It's just that their primary relationship was with alcohol rather than with their children. Penelope spent her time taking care of the younger children and distracting herself from her fear and resentment.

*Andrew was an only child. His parents drank, too; no matter, though, because he was raised by a live-in nanny. He was privileged and over-indulged. Anything he wanted, he got, so his parents didn't have to deal with his attitude. Even as an adult, Andrew never worked a day because of his sizable trust fund. Not only did Andrew see himself as the center of the universe, he believed he **was** the universe. With their respective histories, Penelope and Andrew became a match made in hell. Penelope had no life, so becoming part of Andrew's universe became an easy fit. Penelope gave, and gave, and gave, until there was nothing left* *of her. Andrew took, and took, and took, and still he maintained it wasn't enough. His entitlement was profound.*

When Penelope came for counseling, the thought of letting go of Andrew put her into an existential crisis. If Penelope wasn't taking care of someone else, there was nothing at all to her identity. There was only her perceived void, and it terrified her. She had never looked within to recognize her own needs, only the needs of others.

We worked with her first by revealing her history, and Penelope was able to identify her Impasse of feeling abandoned and afraid at a very early time in her life. That abandonment really broke her spirit, and the neural pathways to her higher mind were blocked. She began to operate from fear at a very early age.

Penelope worked to release her past by relinquishing her judgment that she was not worthy of her parents' regard—the precursor to her own identity. She learned that her parents' alcoholism wasn't good or bad; it just was, and it had nothing to do with her. Penelope began to shift her thinking.

You can change your perception any time you choose to relinquish judgment of the past. When you relinquish judgment, you have released it.

You may have a self-definition that is based on what those who cared for you told you directly or indirectly about who you were. If you were told over and over that you were smart, stupid, industrious, lazy, indecisive, impulsive, headstrong, hard-headed, clumsy, graceful, fat, skinny, a sissy, a jock, etc., these remarks could have become a foundation for your identity. They may have gotten in the way of your fulfillment in exploring and discovering *on your own* who you wanted to be and what was important to you. Imagine if you were free of those judgments and intrusions into your development. Who would you be? How might you choose to define yourself? Who would help bring those characteristics out in you? What type of person would you be drawn to? We don't think it would be a loser.

Write down a detailed description of your authentic self. Who are you? What are you like? What do you do? What is non-negotiable in your life? What are your minimum standards, not only for yourself, but also for the partners you choose? We believe that once you have released the past and you get back into your own body, you will be overjoyed at who you see.

Now we realize that you may be stuck at the Impasse, and we hear the balking. "Right, ladies, my mother made me go out and cut off my own switch from a tree and sit in my room with it, waiting for her to beat me with it, and I have a faulty perception of the event." Yes, your mother did make you get your own weapon of torture, wait until she came, and then beat you with it. And it appears she is still doing it. Only now, she has your permission to do so. You see, the beating itself no longer exists. The beating hurt you physically at the time it happened. It was very painful. Today, only your perception of it remains. Try to grasp this concept. The beating itself never had any meaning. ***The way you felt about yourself at the time it happened imparts the only remaining meaning the beating has***. How did you feel when you were being beaten? Afraid? Sad? Shameful? Angry? What have you done about these feelings? One thing you've done is distract yourself from them by focusing all your attention on cleaning up another person's garbage instead of tidying up your own. Another thing is that you haven't been able to release this particular aspect of your past and move forward. You may have projected these feelings onto other important people or relationships in your life. These distracting behaviors detract from the loving quality of your significant relationships, and don't solve the problem of the underlying pain onto which you hold. Once again we repeat: relinquish your judgment of a scary memory and you have released that memory. Being beaten by your mother was bad when she did it, but it isn't bad now, because it isn't happening now. It just was.

Forgiveness is for people, not for actions.

You may tend to blame your parents for the misery you continue to experience as an adult. You are at risk to see yourself as a victim and start to believe that unless your parents fix it or apologize, you remain forever at the mercy of their crimes. That is when you turn your attention to other people's problems to distract yourself from your feelings of fear and powerlessness. But are you powerless now? Consider this. It's not about your parents anymore. Now it is all about you and your perceptions of them, and yourself in relation to them. Continuing to blame or judge parents, or anyone else for that matter, is just another distraction from your chronic fear. Penelope could spend a lifetime blaming her mother and father for abandoning her and causing her great fear and anxiety. She could blame them for her choice of losers and for taking away her childhood innocence and giftedness. Or, she could choose to forgive them, thereby releasing *herself* from the stronghold these memories have on her life.

How do you change your fearful perceptions of past events so that you can release them and reconnect to the power of your spirit? Through forgiveness, that's how.

Forgiveness, **the relinquishment of judgment followed by a thought of peace,** is the path to recovery from attracting losers and maintaining a cycle of suffering. Without forgiveness, you will always be stopped at your Impasse, finding it impossible to connect to your spirit and your higher mind. For Penelope, it was realizing that she had always been deserving of loving parents, even though she lived with two active alcoholics. She recognized that as long as she carried her childhood fear of them in the here and now, she could never move forward to realize her gifts and talents, and she would stay with losers who would continue to replay this historical scene. As long as she kept inspiring, or breathing life into the memory, she continued to dance the Toxic Tango of Fear. Penelope worked on forgiving her parents by relinquishing her judgment of her parents' alcoholic abandoning behavior, and thinking about them with peace. She also forgave herself for mistakenly believing she was an unlovable child because of the parents she was born to.

Sometimes, forgiveness means
letting go and moving on.

How do you relinquish judgment of someone else or yourself for a painful mistake? Ask yourself this question: "How would I know this differently if I considered it from a position of love rather than of fear?" In other words, "How would my spirit have me know this?" The pain of a scary childhood event can be overwhelming from a position of fear. It can also disappear when you release it with forgiveness.

Forgiveness is for people, not for actions. When you are faced with an awful mistake, be it your own or someone else's, it would be far more effective to forgive yourself and/or the other, and give the mistake over to your higher mind. This relinquishment invites wisdom in to handle the problem. When forgiveness is practiced in this manner, watch the course of events that follow work in a way to rectify the mistake. The same holds true for picking losers to fill our own voids. Sometimes, forgiveness means letting go and moving on.

At this point, we feel it is important for you to consider and chronicle your relationship history. Many times your first "love" sets the minimum standard for all other relationships to follow. Is that the standard you want to keep? What are your minimum relationship standards? These can be powerful, and can strongly influence what you are willing to accept in life. We call this particular dance the Love Limbo; how low will you go?

Minimizing Maya

Maya was a 32-year-old woman who came to us for a consultation, stating that her biological clock was ticking, and she didn't understand why she was having so much trouble finding and maintaining a relationship. She had at least 3 long-term relationships that had all gone the same way; the guy would move in with her, and take over, but would never be willing to take the relationship to the next level—marital commitment. Maya felt like a loser and really believed she was going to miss the boat in her part of the female American dream; love, marriage, children, and the house with a white picket fence. When we asked her to chronicle her relationship history, she noticed for the first time that there was a common theme: she would always let the man set the tone for the relationship, and she would follow blindly.

Her first boyfriend adored football. He bought season tickets for the football games even though she was not a fan. She would go to every one of them in order to spend time with him. She blew off doing things that she enjoyed.

The second man was into classical music and she was not. She would endure hours of this music blasting throughout the house, and never listened to the music she liked, even alone in her car.

The third man loved sushi and dragged her to sushi restaurants on a weekly basis, even though the thought of raw fish made her gag. What really scared her was that when he left, and she went to the mall to shop in an attempt to make herself feel better, she found herself instead wandering aimlessly from store to store, clueless about what appealed to her. That telling experience really opened her eyes to the fact that she was in complete disconnect.

Maya revealed her history. Her parents divorced when she was fifteen years old, and it came as a complete surprise to her. There was never any arguing, fighting or conflict; in fact, her parents appeared to get along beautifully. Her mother was very passive and her father ran the show.

Ultimately, her father left her mother after 16 years of marriage, claiming that his wife had no personality and brought nothing to the table. He told Maya that he had no respect for her mother, who constantly caved in to his every wish and demand, never having an original thought or feeling of her own.

Maya was always looking for her father's approval and always wanted to be what he wanted her to be. He wanted her to take classical piano lessons; she took the lessons, even though she really wanted to play the flute. He wanted her to be involved in team sports; she joined the soccer league, even though she wanted to play tennis. She never developed her own sense of self; she was always what her father wanted her to be.

Maya recognized her Impasse as her fear of abandonment; when her father left her mother, in Maya's mind, he left her as well. She sought out men who continued to leave her because she never brought herself to the table. She was so busy being what she thought they wanted her to be that they never had any idea of who she really was as a person.

Maya grieved the loss of her father, who left through no fault of her own, and worked on relinquishing judgment of herself. She had always mistakenly believed that if she was more of the daughter her father needed her to be, he would have remained in the family with her and her mother, instead of leaving and starting over with another woman and her children. She also worked on forgiving her mother for providing her with very poor role modeling of how to function in a relationship. Once she did this, she was able to move forward and begin to re-invent herself—only this time, she was running the show.

Take some time now and reflect upon a memory that has resulted in a negative self-judgment. It does not necessarily need to be as dramatic as some of the examples that were used in this book in order to illustrate a particular point. Maybe someone in your past contributed to the story of your identity by helping you to believe you are something that you would prefer not to be. You can shift your perception of that memory right now by stating, "That memory is not bad. It just is." Now ask yourself, "How do I feel about myself in this relationship?" If the answer is *incompetent, unhappy, exhausted* or *sad*, then this isn't a relationship at all. Releasing the past through the relinquishment of judgment begins breaking down your Impasse and opening the pathways to your spirit or your higher mind. Now, you are ready to use thoughts of peace to stop picking losers when you are being challenged by fear.

CHAPTER FIVE

Just Say "No" to Losers, or Responding to Fear

Responding and reacting are two different behaviors. They originate from different places in your brain. Reacting involves little or no spiritual connection. It is automatic and falls into the neuro-circuitry of your lower brain's functioning. Reactions are defensive in nature and are based on your primitive instincts of fight or flight. You react when you have a need to protect yourself. Sometimes this is desirable. If someone has their hand clenched in a fist, drawn back in stance of attack, you need to react by getting yourself immediately out of the way. You wouldn't say, "It looks like you are going to hit me. Is this true?" That takes way too long, and you'll certainly end up with a black eye or worse. In situations where you are immediately threatened, the fight or flight instinct kicks in automatically. Reaction skills are very useful should you find yourself in physically dangerous circumstances.

The thoughtful preparation of a reply is called responding. How do you respond in fearful relationship conditions? Do you try to manage the other person? Do you yell at them? Do you shut down and change the subject? Do you avoid attending to those emotionally-charged situations by putting off what is inevitable? If you learn to respond, rather than react, in scary relationship circumstances, you will not need to fight or flee. You will be able to remain present and accountable.

The thoughtful preparation of a reply is called responding.

Responding to fear rather than reacting to it supports your release of the past. Once you have relinquished negative self-judgment originating from your relationships with your parents, you are empowered to stay internally peaceful and are better able to make satisfying partner choices, rather than attracting people who consistently trigger your fear.

You have already committed to letting go of the past. You have committed to no longer perceiving yourself as a victim of it. When fear is triggered you can now recognize that you are at your Impasse. You can choose to rise above your separation anxiety, and can remember that you are not abandoned and that you are not alone. With that in mind, you are not looking for someone else to complete you. You now look for someone who complements you; someone who accepts you for who you are, and you do the same for them. This is called bringing out the best in each other.

Your spiritual self is showing up in the relationship; not your fear-driven, scared little child. Your spiritual self is confidently showing up with authenticity, courage, peace and faith in your ability to build intimacy and commitment.

Have you ever felt afraid or insecure in a relationship? What is that fear about? Why are you afraid? Take some time right now to think about the answers to these questions and to write them down.

Emotional reacting occurs as a result of poor impulse control.

What gut-level reactions do you get into so you don't have to feel the fear? Emotional reacting occurs as a result of poor impulse control. Your immediate impulse is to get away from the scary feeling because it is unpleasant. You impulsively turn to managing the other, which gives fear power over the relationship. We believe that fear and love cannot exist in the same place and have a positive outcome.

You also abandon yourself when you spend all of your time focusing on and reacting to the dysfunction of the other. This dishonors what you are really feeling. You end up treating yourself far worse than the loser treats you! You keep trying to control the other person; but since it is impossible to control another person, you keep coming out of that fear-based exercise in futility seeing yourself as incompetent and a loser! Yuck! Who needs that?

If you acknowledge your fear, instead of running from it, then you can respond rather than react to it. Responding is a discipline and it requires a lot of practice to become good at it. Responding to fear is best developed by following three behavioral steps: Stop, Look and Listen. Do you remember learning this phrase as a child when learning to cross the street? Some streets may be easier to cross than others. How many streets have you crossed where you never bothered to stop, look and listen? At some of the scary intersections, you could be easily mowed down if you didn't adhere to the rule. When you find yourself at a frightening emotional intersection, the rule of responding is to Stop! Look! And Listen!

Let's start with Stop. Identify what will become your personal red light. When you are dating or in a relation-ship with someone, and you become triggered, your historical fear becomes activated and you may not recog-nize this as fear. Your red light might be a gnawing feeling in the pit of your stomach; the hair might stand up on the back of your neck; you might turn to a bad habit; you might even feel yourself becoming depressed; you may become very perfectionistic; or you might procrastinate and avoid tending to important things in your own life. Your work life might start to suffer, or you may start ignoring your children. You have gotten yourself so deep into managing or fixing the other that you don't even notice it anymore. It's like breathing out and breathing in.

Ironically, you will find yourself at a place where your distraction becomes your greatest reminder to respond, rather than react, to what is going on. Pay attention to yourself for a change!

Bloodied Beth

Beth and Ron dated all through high school. She was attracted to him in part because he was a "bad boy," and she had a rebellious side to her, having been raised by a rigid police officer. Ron was a rebel who abused alcohol and drugs, got into minor fights, and was often suspended from school. When they were young, these antics seemed minor to her. Ron had nothing going on after high school, so he signed up as a Marine and was deployed to the Middle East. Beth married him as soon as he had his orders, and she vowed to be faithful to him while he was gone.

The real trouble started when he came home after his tour of duty. One day, he started interrogating her about what she had been up to and whom she had been with while he was gone. Even though she asserted that she had been faithful to him while he was gone, he continued his intimidating and threatening style of inquisition. Finally, he cornered her in the living room, screaming at her, "Tell me the truth, you bitch!" Then he slapped her across the face, and blood started to pour out her nose.

Beth ran out and found refuge at her parents' house. She told her parents that she'd walked into a door, but they didn't believe her. They immediately took her to the hospital emergency room, and while she was being admitted, her parents summoned the hospital social worker, hoping that Beth would tell her what they believed was the true tale. When the social worker asked Beth about what had happened, she stuck by her original story; that she'd walked into a door.

After the hospital patched her up, Beth returned home to Ron, who apologized profusely. He fell to his knees and begged her forgiveness, promising it would never happen again. Beth believed him, because she so wanted to. Internally, she came up with all sorts of excuses to justify his violent outburst.

This first "honeymoon period" lasted about six weeks before it cycled again…and again….and again. With each repetition, each honeymoon period became shorter and shorter, and Beth became like putty in the hands of her abuser.

Beth finally ended up at a local battered women's shelter and was referred to us for counseling. She revealed her history with Ron, and then began talking about her life growing up. Her father was militant in his role as a parent. He believed that children should *abide by a very stringent set of rules, and if they strayed from the path, the punishment was swift and severe. Beth's father never hit her; he never had to. One look was enough to instill the fear. Her mother was almost unconscious when it came to parenting. She was like a robot in her daily activities. She cooked, cleaned, made beds and shopped for food, but when it came to interacting, she was barely there. The best word Beth could use to describe her mother was numb. It made her cry.*

Beth identified her Impasses as a fear of being hit and a fear of being hurt. She erroneously learned early on that someone else's rage was her problem rather than their own. She falsely believed that if she was better-behaved, her father would be nicer. When she met her husband in high school, she had originally perceived him as a breath of fresh air in his rebelliousness; as being something she dared not be. She paid little attention to Ron's possessiveness and domination. She was flattered by it and mistakenly justified those behaviors to mean that he must really love her. Bad call.

The first thing we had to help her to understand was that she had picked a loser, and had let herself become brainwashed by him. He did this in a number of ways: by threatening her; by presenting himself as having all the power; by helping her to believe there was no way out of the relationship with him; by isolating her. He would check up on her constantly and not let her have any outside relationships, and throw her an occasional crumb, where he would be nice for a minute or two; just long enough to feed into her denial system of, "You see, he's changing. He's calming down."

Beth was able to forgive her father for his scariness and she gave him back the shame of his rage and anger. It wasn't hers, and she wasn't going to carry it another second. She also forgave her mother for abandoning and betraying her through failing to protect her. She forgave herself for having believed that she ever deserved to be on the receiving end of verbal, emotional or physical violence. Her personal red light became the phrase, "Calm down, Ron." As soon as she heard herself say that to Ron, or to anyone else for that matter, she knew she had to stop and listen to what was going on within. She would allow herself to feel that fear and rise above it through more positive self-talk.

Eventually, Beth got an order of protection against Ron and filed for divorce. When he came knocking on her door, she called the police and had him arrested. Ron soon came to find out that Beth wasn't putting up with his garbage another second. He got involved in an anger management program, started on antidepressant medication, and over the course of one year, they were able to work things out with the assistance of a marital counselor. Once Beth saw that Ron took responsibility for his behavior and was committed to treating his own emotional disorder, she was able to see that he was no longer a loser, and she began to appreciate the fun qualities and positive parts of his personality that had attracted her to him in the first place.

Keep this advice in mind when you are identifying your personal red light: never tell yourself things like, "I don't know," or "I'm trying," as you begin to develop this skill. The statements "I don't know," and "I'm trying," are very popular distractions to avoid dealing with fear. They are actually a serious form of self-abandonment that will keep you stuck in the victim position, will strengthen your Impasse, and will leave you feeling powerless and hopeless. There is really no such thing as "trying" when you are making choices for positive change. You are either doing it or not doing it. You don't have to be hard on yourself when you are not doing it, but at least be honest about it.

> *There is really no such thing*
> *as "trying" when you are making choices*
> *for positive change.*

When you ask yourself the hard questions about why you pick losers, the answer, "I don't know," is only reinforcing your underlying struggle of unworthiness, and it undermines your ability to respond to fear. Of course you know why, but if you admitted to it, then you would have to take on the responsibility of making a healthy change. If you're afraid to look at why, simply say so as your first powerful step. Stop and honor your feeling of fear. It is okay, and it makes perfect sense that you would experience fear in letting go.

You always know in your heart of hearts what is going on with you. Stuck at the Impasse, you might be afraid to look at it. Once you have stopped your denial and responded to your historical fear, you free yourself to look inward and reveal your truth in what is happening. Again, we ask you the questions, "Why are you holding yourself hostage with this person?" "What are you afraid of?" "Do you really think you would shrivel up and die if you let go of them?" Now listen to your truth. Please don't answer with, "I don't know." You do know. Just take some time and sit with your feelings long enough to really feel them. Just stay present for yourself. If you would just have your feelings, they won't have you. Listen to your answer. It deserves to be heard. And remember, you can't lose what you don't have.

Troubled Tom

Tom was an insurance salesman who made a moderate but adequate living. His wife was the high-powered CFO of a major international corporation, and made an extraordinary amount of money, making her the major breadwinner of the family. They lived in a very high-end neighborhood. Their two boys attended the best private schools. They wanted for nothing, and his wife never let Tom forget it. When she wasn't working or attending power-based social functions, she was emasculating her husband.

Tom came into counseling very deep in his role as a victim, but he didn't recognize it as such. Over the years, his wife had so broken his spirit that he had no confidence in himself. Basically, he saw himself as worthless and of no use to anyone. He felt paralyzed. He didn't want to stay in the marriage, but he couldn't leave, fearing that no one else would want such a loser.

Tom revealed his history, and realized on some level that he'd married his father, a powerful government official who prided himself on how important he was, and how unimportant his wife's contributions to the marriage were. Tom recalled frequent interactions during his childhood where his father spoke in a demeaning tone to Tom's mother. Tom's mother appeared to just ignore the comments. She focused on the children and on her church activities, which included numerous missions to third-world countries. Tom recalled feeling terrified when she left; he really worried that she wouldn't come back. After all, who would want to come back to being treated that way?

Tom identified his Impasses as fear of abandonment, fear of incompetence, and fear of not being lovable. He worked to forgive his father for his overbearing, nasty, and arrogant manner, realizing that his parents' toxic relationship just was the way it was. It had nothing to do with Tom's value and lovability.

Tom was able to release his past. He then identified what his personal stop light would be when his wife treated him in a way that triggered his childhood fear of being unlovable. His red light became a warm flush of shame he would feel in his body when she spoke to him in her negative, condescending manner. He practiced speaking his truth, which was to say to his wife, "Honey, I don't like the way I feel when you speak to me like this. I feel incompetent and I need to feel good about myself in our marriage. I am requesting that you pay attention to how you speak to me, and by doing so, our relationship can grow and we can have more positive outcomes."

Unfortunately, she never honored his request, so he finally told her he wanted a divorce. His wife made a 180 degree turn, begging him to stay. She promised she would stop, but it was too late. He was done with the marriage, and in the end, she was the loser.

For Tom, looking into his fear told him that he deserved positive regard and respect, and that he was lovable. If you look back at all the relationship challenges described in the stories of this book, their one common thread is unfinished parental business. When these people revealed their history, recognized their particular Impasse of fear, released their past, and responded to fear, they were either able to greatly improve their existing relationship, or to let it go through forgiveness and move on to a healthier and more fulfilling relationship. Look into your fear. What is it telling you about yourself? Listen. Write it down.

Stop, look and listen is a precious opportunity to take a look within. As you do this, think about some aspects of your identity that you really don't like. When you choose losers, you are creating a mirror of this perceived lost part of yourself.

If you are unhappy in your present relationship, ask yourself these questions: "What is this person showing me about myself? In what ways do I see myself as a loser? Am I a loser; is that really a true remark?" Please, stop saying that. Stop judging yourself. Do you remember that judgments only serve to keep you entrenched in the painful part of your past? When you are in a responding mode, you can ask yourself, "What do I want to create for myself? Is this the way I want to see myself? What would I create instead?" Write down all the answers to these questions. Go slowly and give yourself some time and put some thought into the process.

Consider acknowledging and responding to your inner fear. You are now empowered to notice it, reframe it as an Impasse, and then identify the judgment you have cast upon yourself because of it. When you are on the brink of engaging in a losing relationship, **stop, look and listen**. You can then patiently identify what it is you need in order to be at peace and free of fear. Now, go for it.

CHAPTER SIX

What Was Lost Is Found,
or Reconnecting To Your Spirit

Reconnecting to your spirit is finding all that was precious and innocent in you once again. Here is your moment of truth, the chance to know who you really are and to be authentic in your relationships. Once you have completed the first four steps, this one is simple. You have relinquished judgment of yourself and others. You have used thoughts of peace and given over your fear to your spirit or higher mind. You are now ready to be one with your higher self.

This is the only step that requires you to do almost nothing! Just be still and calmly listen. Simply be present for yourself. You are no longer invested in distracting yourself by managing the negative parts of someone else's personality. Having identified your historical grievances, you have moved beyond separation anxiety and you are ready to be present in a relationship to receive as well as to give.

This requires no concerted effort on your part except a calm, attentive, listening position. The people who will bring out the best in you are well within your reach. It is as if you attract them into your life. You are ready to be intimate with yourself and another, and with practice, you learn to remember who you are. Spiritually-based attributes become the core of your identity.

> *The people who will bring out the best*
> *in you are well within your reach.*

Reconnecting to your spirit implies that you have released your past and have responded to your fears as you applied the two steps of forgiveness. When you practice this over time, forgiveness tends to come to mind quickly and doesn't require much effort on your part. Think about how much energy you have poured into managing others—energy that you can now direct into more productive states in yourself such as trust, honesty, tolerance, gentleness, joy, self-intimacy, generosity, patience, faithfulness, and open-mindedness. First you get to enjoy these characteristics for yourself. This will feel so wonderfully liberating and powerful that you will be enthusiastic to extend the same to others. You then will be able to co-create healthy spiritual alliances.

Initially, when you reconnect to your spirit and seem to be doing just fine, something will happen that will typically shoot you down and leave you vulnerable to relapse into your old behaviors. When you begin to make your shift to the higher mind, you may first experience an intensification of fear as a way to bring you back to the familiarity of your prior distress and distraction. You might find yourself being seduced by fear to slip back into the distraction of managing others. At these times, you can explore and discover a vehicle for looking within to help you stay present and authentic.

Here are some activities, other than meditation or prayer, which might work as ways to calm your mind and help you to look within:

- Practicing yoga
- Being in nature
- Engaging in the arts
- Playing sports
- Sending peace to the person you dislike
- Reading and journaling
- Cooking a meal
- Stargazing
- Helping the sick
- Doing charitable acts
- Taking care of children
- Playing games

- Needlepoint, knitting or crocheting
- Helping the elderly
- Reading for the blind
- Participating in an ecological endeavor
- Joining or forming a support group
- Actively listening
- Expressing gratitude

These are just some suggestions. You may have your own ideas in mind.

Here are the relationship re-creations that were addressed in this book:

An endearing behavior — Willie reminded Emma of a very fond paternal behavior. This strengthened their relationship and enhanced the affection between them.

Perfectionistic standards — Rena's fear of inadequacy had its roots in a shaming, critical father, and she had unconsciously assumed his role in her relationship with Michael. She brought him in for counseling, where they practiced creating a more positive relationship style.

Managing another's emotional disorder — Martin witnessed his mother manage his father's personality disorder over the years and realized he was recreating this in his love life. He turned his caretaking ways toward becoming a Big Brother, which allowed his wife to take responsibility for her own personal struggles.

Bullying — Billy covered his anxiety with nasty, threatening, and intimidating behavior. When he backed up to the anxious, wounded little boy behind the bully, he stopped. His behavior and his relationship greatly improved.

Abdicating Power — Lisa's fear of not being lovable enough attracted those who would not respect her boundaries. Lisa learned to extend the courtesy of informing Bryan 20 minutes before she intended to leave for an event. If he was not ready, she would leave on her own. After 3 repetitions of this, Bryan was always ready on time.

People Pleasing — Penelope maintained control by making other people dependent on her so that they would never leave her. She worked to get in touch with her separation anxiety and re-directed her need to be nice to places where it truly helped, such as local charity organizations. She divorced Andrew and met a wonderful man who was able to give and receive in the relationship.

No Personal Identity — Maya never developed a self of self, so she never really showed up in a relationship. She took some time to redevelop herself by attending a weekend retreat for personal growth. She still attends the ongoing support group.

Carried Feelings — Beth preemptively carried the shameful feelings of her violent partner and was invested in managing his rage. She began to let him experience the consequences of his own poor behavioral choices. His behaviors improved and she began to like what she saw in him.

Victim Mentality — Tom was invested in seeing himself

as a victim so he wouldn't have to face his fear of taking responsibility for his own independence. He divorced his wife and literally started over at square one regarding his career, his home and a new relationship. He remained in counseling through this process, so that he could remain empowered to build the type of life that he deserved.

When life's challenges trigger your historical upsets, you are at risk of feeling afraid and then distracting yourself by managing others. When you remember forgiveness, **the relinquishment of judgment followed with a thought of peace,** you can notice your fear, rise above it to your spiritual perspective, remain centered, and stay strong in your ability to **STOP PICKING LOSERS!**

We wish you luck.

Ellie and Vicki

PART TWO

The Rapid Advance Workbook
To Just Stop Picking Losers!

CONTENTS

Part Two:
The Rapid Advance Workbook

INTRODUCTION

We have been in the *helping* professions collectively for over 50 years. We have helped countless people face their relationship challenges as well as facing our own. We all deserve to feel happy and fulfilled in our relationships and too many of us put up with unnecessary pain for too long.

The Rapid Advance Process offered in this workbook will be the beginning of the most positive change in your life! Working it will help you see yourself as whole and free from the pain of loss, so you can stop picking losers. This workbook follows the book **Just Stop Picking Losers: The Rapid Advance Process for Attracting Loving Relationships**, which is an important resource for anyone who wants a happy and fulfilling love life. Please be sure to read the book before starting the workbook.

Now, follow along with us; take your time; and use this guide in a way that will best serve your individual needs.

CHAPTER ONE

Looking At Yourself As A Person

Do you feel internally calm and peaceful enough to handle the challenges of a relationship?

_____

_____

_____

_____

Has anything traumatic happened to you in your life? (It doesn't have to be some big dramatic event. Remember, trauma is in the eye of the beholder.)

_____

_____

_____

_____

_____

_____

What does the word *spirituality* mean to you?

_____

_____

_____

_____

What puts a lump in your throat, or makes you really emotional?

_____

_____

_____

_____

Are you feeling satisfied with your family connections?

_____

_____

_____

_____

_____

_____

Are you suffering from any chronic or intermittent unexplained physical symptoms?

_____

_____

_____

_____

Are you sleeping well?

_____

_____

_____

_____

Do you worry?

_____

_____

_____

_____

Are you happy?

_____

_____

_____

_____

Do you make time for your own personal enjoyment?

_____

_____

_____

_____

What do you do to relax?

_____

_____

_____

_____

Do you think you can really get close to someone?

_____

_____

_____

_____

Do you want someone to get really close to you?

_____

_____

_____

_____

If you let someone get really close to you, what do you think (or fear) they would find out about you? Think about this question and write your truthful answer.

_____

_____

_____

_____

_____

_____

EXERCISE 1:

An Act of Courage

Write down five issues that seem to constantly come up for you in relationships.

1. _____

2. _____

3. _____

4. _____

5. _____

EXERCISE 2:

An Act of Faith

Write down five things that would be different and better for you if you allowed yourself to build your own confidence and sense of emotional independence.

1. _____
2. _____
3. _____
4. _____
5. _____

Rapid Advance Technique

We have come to understand that the underlying dynamic of picking losers is your own denied sense that on some level, **you** are the loser. We also have reframed this sense of "loss" as the loss of connectedness to your higher mind or spiritual self. When we are operating from our spiritual self, we are not afraid, and do not see ourselves as alone. We are then empowered to attract healthy love that helps us to heal, rather than hurt.

Before we embark on this journey of recovery, let's first clear your mind of any negative or counterproductive notions of spirituality. Many of us were raised with religious practices that were either heavy-handed or forced upon us. Others were raised with no spiritual practice at all. Some of us have simply allowed that part of our experience to waste away over time.

EXERCISE 1:

List any negative connotations that the word *spirituality* elicits for you.

_____

_____

_____

_____

EXERCISE 2:

Make a list of the traits, characteristics, and behaviors you would like to create as you become more spiritual in your relationships.

_____   _____

_____   _____

_____   _____

_____   _____

What would that part of you feel like?

_____

_____

_____

_____

How would that part be of assistance to you when you
are in a relationship? Please do not rush through this
segment.

_____

_____

_____

_____

_____

_____

_____

_____

_____

_____

_____

We are now ready to proceed with the Rapid Advance
Process. By completing the next five chapters you will
have the opportunity to mend, build and strengthen a
strong connection to yourself. In so doing, you will have
the opportunity to develop a reliable practice of accessing
your own remarkable internal resources.

The Rapid Advance Process consists of five steps for relationship revitalization:

1. **Reveal Your History**
2. **Recognize Your Impasse**
3. **Release Your Past**
4. **Respond to Your Fear**
5. **Reconnect with Your Spirit**

Please remember, this is not a substitute for treatment for recovered memories of traumatizing events earlier in one's life. This process is for relationship health. If you are an adult survivor of serious <u>untreated</u> childhood trauma, it is imperative that you obtain appropriate treatment for your psychological injuries.

CHAPTER THREE

Reveal Your History: *It Was*

You may think that your history contains nothing significant that triggers or upsets you. Nonetheless, a part of
your brain relays every memory you ever experienced,
and at the most inopportune times. Whether your
fears from childhood are a dark closet, being bullied by
a scary child, getting caught in the rain, coming home
from school and having no one in the house, hearing
strange noises, having nightmares, losing a friend, losing
a love, accidents, feeling publicly embarrassed in school
or in front of the family, becoming ill and missing out
on important activities, surgery, hospital stays, shyness,
or moving, just to name a few; they are stored. These

"historical feeling states" can be triggered in our present-day relationships. Having an awareness of your historical hot buttons is crucial in the maintenance of your emotional and spiritual well-being in relationships.

EXERCISE 1:

The following questions will help build your awareness of historical feeling states and/or experiences that may seem to be normal events to you, but may get triggered in the course of your relationships. You may also have significant recollection of events but you may not have an awareness of the body memories and the gut-feelings associated with these memories. You may even think you have dealt with some of these memories and laid them to rest. We now ask you to reconsider them in this new context. Doing so may help you to stop picking losers.

As you move through the exercises below, be patient. Go slowly and become introspective in a gentle and self-accepting manner. The purpose of revealing your history is not to judge or evaluate; it is simply to honor and acknowledge.

YOUR PARENTS, YOUR FAMILY AND YOUR WORDLY ATTACHMENTS

Describe your early memories of your mother with five adjectives:

1. _____
2. _____
3. _____
4. _____
5. _____

Describe your early memories of your father with five adjectives:

1. _____
2. _____
3. _____
4. _____
5. _____

Did your family suffer a life altering event such as a death or divorce? How was this addressed?

_____
_____
_____
_____

_____

_____

If you lived in a blended family system, describe the dynamics associated with this experience.

_____

_____

_____

_____

_____

_____

Imagine watching an old movie of yourself as a child. Describe what you see.

_____

_____

_____

_____

_____

_____

Describe your parents' marriage with five adjectives:

1. _____

2. _____

3. _____

4. _____

5. _____

How did your parents/step-parents resolve their conflicts?
What did you see? What did you hear or not hear?

_____

_____

_____

_____

_____

_____

How did you feel when your parents/step-parents were
having conflicts?

_____

_____

_____

_____

_____

_____

How did you feel when conflicts went unaddressed?

_____

_____

_____

_____

_____

_____

How did your parents/step-parents handle issues around money?

_____

_____

_____

_____

_____

_____

How did your parents/step-parents handle issues around religion?

_____

_____

_____

_____

How did your parents/step-parents handle issues around food?

_____

_____

_____

_____

_____

_____

How did your family have fun together?

_____

_____

_____

_____

_____

_____

How was affection displayed in your family?

_____

_____

_____

_____

_____

_____

How were issues around sex approached in your family?

_____

_____

_____

_____

_____

_____

How was illness addressed in your family?

_____

_____

_____

_____

_____

_____

Was there any addiction or substance abuse in your family? How did it you affect you?

_____

_____

_____

_____

_____

_____

What was the role of extended family?

_____

_____

_____

_____

_____

_____

How were you disciplined?

_____

_____

_____

_____

_____

_____

How were your relationships with your siblings? What was your birth order?

_____

_____

_____

_____

_____

_____

What are your most vivid memories?

_____

_____

_____

_____

_____

_____

What were your greatest joys as a child?

_____

_____

_____

_____

_____

_____

What scared you as a child?

_____

_____

_____

_____

_____

_____

What were some ways you used to distract yourself when you felt afraid or upset? Some examples might be day-dreaming, thumb sucking, nail biting, masturbating, nightmares, bed wetting, temper tantrums, withdrawal, bullying, underachieving, over-achieving, lying or crying.

_____

_____

_____

_____

_____

_____

How did you get attention?

_____

_____

_____

_____

_____

_____

Did you have any behavioral problems as a child? If so,
what were they?

_____

_____

_____

_____

_____

Did you have any particular challenges in growing up that
stand out in your memory, such as poverty, illness, learning disabilities, disappointments, deaths, divorce, etc?

_____

_____

_____

_____

_____

_____

YOUR EDUCATIONAL EXPERIENCES

Describe your experience in elementary school.

_____

_____

_____

_____

_____

_____

Describe your experience in middle school.

_____

_____

_____

_____

_____

_____

Describe your experience in high school.

_____

_____

_____

_____

_____

_____

Did you change schools while you were growing up? If so, how often?

_____

_____

_____

_____

_____

_____

If you moved, how did it affect your relationships?

_____

_____

_____

_____

_____

_____

How did your parents explain the moves?

_____

_____

_____

_____

_____

_____

How did your family communicate about important life changes?

_____

_____

_____

_____

_____

_____

Describe any other significant relationships that you had while growing up: friendships, romances, relationships with grandparents, aunts, uncles, teachers or other authority figures, peer groups, extracurricular activities you participated in, etc.

_____

_____

_____

_____

_____

_____

EXERCISE 2:

Write the story of your first love. Keep it detailed.

_____

_____

_____

_____

_____

_____

_____

_____

_____

_____

_____

_____

_____

_____

_____

_____

EXERCISE 3:

What patterns do you see emerging as you reveal certain aspects of your history? How you developed and evolved is important to how you cope today. Our goal here is to find patterns that become identifiable to you. Examples of patterns that you may acknowledge are Avoidant, Passive, Aggressive, Passive-Aggressive, Abusive, Neglectful, Overprotective, Depressed, Anxious, Disconnected, Numb, Silent, Addictive, Oppositional, Bystanding, Perfectionistic, etc. You may come up with a pattern of your own that is not mentioned here. No one knows your history better than you do!

_____

_____

_____

_____

_____

_____

_____

_____

_____

_____

_____

_____

EXERCISE 4:

After revealing your history, identify and write down some judgments, opinions and evaluations you began to make about yourself and your place in the world as you moved through the early developmental stages of life. For example, a child who had a chronically ill mother may have judged themselves as abandoned and alone, or may have seen themselves as a caretaker for that parent, or even as a "stand-in spouse" for the other parent.

Another example is that an adopted child may have frequently felt sad because they judged themselves as an outsider, or perhaps they felt disconnected from the rest of the family. A child of addictive parents may have judged themselves as unworthy of attention and regard because the parents appeared more interested in the addictive substance (e.g. alcohol, drugs, gambling) than they were in the child. A child of divorce may have judged themselves as the cause of the divorce and there-fore, not lovable enough to keep the family intact.

These types of self-judgments, while untrue, are likely conclusions for a child to draw because at an early stage of development, a child naturally tends to perceive him/herself as the center of the universe. It is our wish for you to begin, as adults, to identify and address these faulty core beliefs. Below, write down the judgments you made about yourself as a child growing up in the context of your family.

_____

_____

CHAPTER FOUR

Recognizing Your Impasse: *It Is*

History repeats itself. Even history that we don't recall repeats itself. Revealing your history is an empowering first step. Now we would like you to consider how you might unwittingly re-create some early patterns in your current relationships. We are referring to the patterns that you have already identified in the preceding chapter. Those of us who have unconscious and/or unresolved fears and judgments about ourselves are at risk to repeat the pattern in our romantic relationships.

The Impasse is defined as an emotional and physiological fear reaction; a fear reaction that has its roots in our history. This reaction has three dimensions: 1) the memory itself; 2) the negative feeling you have attached to it; and 3) the judgment you have made about yourself and the others involved in it. When triggered, you continue to distract yourself, believing the distraction to be a form of self-protection, when in reality the only thing that is being protected is the historical fear itself. *The unconscious purpose of defending your Impasse is to protect yourself from ever having to feel the fear that originated in early childhood.* Children normally find ways to distract themselves from feeling afraid simply because fear is an overwhelming feeling state. A child does not yet possess the thinking skills or the internal regulatory tools to manage their fears.

As an adult, rather than resort to distracting behaviors, which are generally destructively; you need to recognize the historical fear, turn into it, and overcome it. Until now, you have used various distractions to avoid feeling afraid. Your goal now is to no longer distract yourself. You deserve and need to recognize the personal distraction you're using which covers your original fear. You are now ready to move into the fear and not into the distraction. Recognize the originating fear and identify it. We will call this your Impasse.

The self-protective distractions of your childhood matured as you developed. Now that you have revealed your history, you are able to recognize and become conscious about how you find yourself at your own Impasse repeatedly in adulthood, and especially in your love relationships.

EXERCISE 1:

Let us recognize how this step applies to you. Think again and repeat the identification of childhood distractions/coping mechanisms you utilized when you felt afraid. List them below.

_____

_____

_____

_____

_____

_____

EXERCISE 2:

Now contemplate the more adult behaviors that you have today that might be considered "evolved distractions" of your childhood reactions to fear. For example, a thumb-sucker or a nail biter may now be a cigarette smoker; a shy child may be a socially withdrawn adult; a child that used illness for attention may be chronically ill as an adult; an overachiever may turn into a workaholic; a bully might grow up to struggle with road rage. List the adult distractions you use below.

_____

_____

_____

_____

_____

_____

_____

_____

_____

When you peel away the distractions, you might notice that you are experiencing anxiety. The anxiety you feel when you stop distracting yourself is a form of separation anxiety, emptiness, or a void resulting from being in disconnect from the spiritual part of your personality. All children have some form of anxiety when they feel afraid, because their little brains have yet to develop the cerebral cortex—that area of the brain that is responsible for higher thinking or rational thought. So you are not alone with this anxiety. Everyone has it in one form or another. Now that you know this, you can move forward and learn how to have it, so that it doesn't have you.

As an adult, you have now developed this part of your brain which needs to be more regularly accessed as a healthy coping mechanism for dealing with fear. Training our brains to move into this higher functioning is derailed when we continue to distract ourselves with childhood coping mechanisms rather than adult responses. Our goal is to open the spiritual bridge or neural pathway to your spiritual mind and that part of your higher brain.

EXERCISE 3:

a. It is now time to think about and write down a relationship situation where you found yourself feeling
   particularly uncomfortable, or that evoked a body
   reaction, anger, or fear in you. Use the space below for
   this exercise.

_____

_____

_____

_____

_____

_____

_____

_____

_____

_____

_____

_____

b. Recognize when you are playing an updated version of
   an historical scene in your relationship, and allow
   yourself to experience rather than avoid the unpleasant separation anxiety that gets triggered in the replay.
   You need to experience your legitimate anxiety in
   order to heal. Write down something from your

personal history that you unconsciously replay over and over in your love relationship.

_____
_____
_____
_____
_____
_____
_____
_____
_____
_____
_____

c. Now say to yourself, "Something is getting triggered in me. This is not about my partner. This is about what my partner's behavior is triggering from my own personal history. It's okay that I am feeling this. I will not judge it. I will remain calm so that I may identify what is coming to the surface. By identifying and becoming conscious of it, I will take better care of myself. I don't have to react the way I did as a child. I am an adult now and I have other choices. I do not have to distract myself from this upset in order to survive. Instead, I need to feel what I am feeling, move through it, and remember that the memory that is being triggered is in the past and does not have to hold any meaning for me in the present. It is powerless over me today." Take time to write down what you're thinking and feeling.

_____

_____

_____

_____

_____

_____

d. Write down the subjects that trigger your Impasses: (Some examples might be childhood violence, molestation, abandonment, corporal punishment, divorce, death of a family member, death of a child, moving, an angry father/mother, a passive mother/father, peer rejection, failure at something we attempted, bullying, cheating, accidents, foul weather, illness, addictions, neglect, certain words, the parental "look", etc.)

_____

_____

_____

_____

_____

_____

e. Put your Impasse into words into the space below. Remember, your Impasse contains your memory of the event, the feelings you had about the event when it happened, and how you judged or evaluated yourself or others involved in light of the event.

_____

_____

_____

_____

_____

_____

_____

_____

_____

_____

_____

No one knows your Impasse better than you. Develop an inner awareness of your Impasse and make friends with it. Don't avoid it any more. Right now we ask you to recognize it so you can move forward and think peacefully about it.

CHAPTER FIVE

Release Your Past: *I Can*

Your unconscious attachment to some parts of your past prohibit you from bridging to the higher mind or spiritual self, which is the most powerful and peaceful part of you. When that part of you is present, you can stay peacefully centered in the here and now. Having identified your Impasse and decided to no longer retreat from it, you can now begin to mend the break in your spiritual bridge. By releasing your painful perception of the past, you can stop protecting an historical fear, and can heal your connection to hope and peacefulness. You are now beginning to successfully connect or bridge to your higher mind and access the power of your spiritual self. This will empower you to create and attract love in your relationships.

In releasing the past you must remember that your memories don't equal the past. What you remember is far less impacting than *how* you remember it. The historical action itself is over. It is only your judgment of yourself and others in its context that remains. For example, if you have a memory of being disciplined by an aggressive parent, there may be a childlike part of you that remembers this event with embarrassment or shame. You may believe, in some way, that you were not worthy of receiving love. The memory itself is far less damaging than your perception or judgment of who you are in light of it. So think of this possibility: when your partner raises his/her voice...bang!! A trigger is tripped for you. You can heal your perception of a painful historical event anytime you choose to relinquish judgment of that event.

EXERCISE 1:

a. Review the historical events that you identified as Impasses.

_____

_____

_____

_____

_____

_____

_____

b. Correlate the feelings you had with those particular Impasse memories. (Painful memories might typically elicit feelings of sadness, embarrassment, shame, disappointment, anger and/or fear. These feelings, unaddressed, may generate a personal sense of inadequacy in you which can be mirrored in the type of person you attract.

_____

_____

_____

_____

_____

_____

c. List the judgments or negative thoughts you made about yourself or others around these Impasse events. For example: "I was a bad girl because my father was always angry," or, "I was unlovable because no one paid attention to me."

_____

_____

_____

_____

_____

_____

_____

EXERCISE 2:

In order to rid yourself of these judgments and faulty beliefs, you now need to exchange your fear for forgiveness.

a. Admit you have the fear. Write down what you are afraid of (for example, I have a fear of not being good enough, of being stupid, embarrassed, etc.)

_____

_____

_____

_____

_____

_____

b. Take personal responsibility for the role your memory is playing in your life and decide what it is that you want to create around this memory. (For example: healing, peace, calmness, closure, release, or forgiveness, versus resentment, anger, hostility, grievance, continued pain, vengeance, depression, anxiety or physical illness.)

_____

_____

_____

_____

_____

_____

c. Realize the negative judgment or faulty thinking that
   you associate with the historical event, and on the
   person or persons in the event with you. List these
   counterproductive thoughts, perceptions, and judgments below.

_____

_____

_____

_____

_____

_____

d. Remove all descriptors (adjectives or adverbs) that
   depict the event. For example, rather than say,
   "My father was a disgusting drunk and I hated him!"
   say instead, "My father drank too much and sometimes I felt afraid of him."

_____

_____

_____

_____

_____

_____

e. Remove all the judgments that you unconsciously made at an earlier time from the description of the event. Commit to exchanging your fear around this event with forgiveness; forgiveness of yourself and forgiveness of the others who were involved. You do not have to forgive the event itself. The event may not have been okay. You are forgiving yourself and the other people involved so that you can be released. Remember, this forgiveness is not for them—it is for **you** to be free. It is through your forgiveness of the other person that you can be released from a painful past. Take time to write down what you're thinking or feeling.

f. Write in the space below, "I forgive..." (e.g. my father for being an alcoholic) and, "I forgive myself for..." (e.g. believing that I wasn't lovable enough for him to stop drinking.)

Forgiveness is for people, not for actions. For example, spanking is an action; the fact that you were spanked doesn't mean that you were bad. Maybe you engaged in behavior that was unacceptable; that doesn't mean that you are unacceptable. You made a mistake; you're not a mistake.

_____

_____

_____

_____

_____

_____

_____

_____

_____

_____

_____

_____

EXERCISE 3:

What stands in your way when you think about forgiveness? (For example, some people see themselves as justified in carrying grievances.)

_____

_____

_____

_____

_____

In deciding to release the past, you can move from fear to forgiveness. Forgiveness is the release of judgment followed by peaceful thoughts. You can now remember that in light of a painful memory, you remain worthy of compassion and regard. The thoughts of peace will now serve you in your next step, responding to fear.

CHAPTER SIX

Respond To Your Fear: *I Know*

There is a big difference between responding and reacting. Reacting involves little or no spiritual connetion. It is based on the primitive brain's instinct of fight, flight or freeze, and is defensive in nature. You react when you perceive the need to protect yourself. If you take yourself back to the first step, you'll remember that you are invested in protecting yourself from feeling historical fears. To do so is faulty thinking and is a dangerous place to put yourself when looking to attract healthy love.

Responding involves the introduction of a reply or an answer and is associated with the conscious left brain. Take a second and consider how you tend to react in emotionally-charged or fearful conditions in your relationships. Some possibilities are perfectionism, procrastination, rage, impatience and silence.

Once you have relinquished or given over the self-judgment you unconsciously made at a much earlier time, you need to stay peaceful when you meet up with yourself in your partner. Responding, rather than reacting, implies thinking peacefully or calmly when you are deciding what to do or what to say in that fear-provoking situation. Responding rather than reacting to emotional fear is the most important part of attracting and maintaining a healthy love. Responding is a discipline. It requires a lot of mental structure and practice in order to become proficient at it.

Now that you have revealed your history, recognized your Impasse and made a commitment to release the past, you are ready to respond to the historical fear that gets triggered through your intimate relationships.

EXERCISE 1:
Stop, Look and Listen

Do you remember learning this phrase as a child when you were learning to cross the street? Some streets are easier to cross than others. At some of the dangerous intersections, you could easily be mowed down if you didn't adhere to the rule. When you find yourself at a scary emotional intersection in your work, the rule of responding is to stop, look and listen.

Stop: Identify what will become your personal red light. What was once a burden in your distraction from fear can now serve you as a blessing, in that it signals that something is being triggered for you. Simply stop. What is your adult distraction when you feel afraid? Here are some possibilities: raging, numbing out, drinking, doing drugs, withdrawing, isolating, stealing, shopping, dissociating, impatience, passivity, eating disorders, working too much, headaches, stomachaches, ringing in the ears, intrusive thoughts, nightmares, sleeping, fuzzy thinking, or forgetting to breathe. What are yours? Keep in mind that it could be more than one symptom.

_____

_____

_____

_____

_____

Look: Look inside, become introspective, and think about what is being triggered in your history. Acknowledge it. Honor it. Relinquish judgment about yourself and others involved. Think peacefully about it. Forgive it. For example, if your father-hunger is being triggered by your partner's abandoning behavior, and you have stopped the distracting behaviors you used to engage in to mask the pain, you have now freed yourself to look inward and reveal your truth as to what is happening.

Listen: Listen to your inner voice and your inner truth.

EXERCISE 2:

a. Write about a time when a lover triggered something deeply personal for you. As you write it, you can listen peacefully to your inner story and remember that this is about *you* and not about what your partner did or didn't do to trigger your upset. The upset belongs to you and you need to be accountable for it. Then, realize that you deserve to forgive, to be forgiven, and to be more patient with yourself and the other. Write your story using "I" statements, and conclude with the statement: "May this story rest in peace."

_____

_____

_____

_____

_____

_____

_____

_____

_____

_____

_____

b. Practice the two forgiveness steps of relinquishing judgment followed by having peaceful thoughts. Write about what you're thinking or feeling.

_____

_____

_____

_____

_____

_____

c. In the space below, make a forgiveness list for hurts you have incurred in your love life. Every story is an opportunity for practicing forgiveness, which has been described for centuries as being divine.

_____

_____

_____

_____

_____

_____

_____

_____

_____

_____

d. Make a list of all the people you want to forgive,
   and also include the things for which you wish to be
   forgiven.

_____

_____

_____

_____

_____

_____

_____

_____

_____

_____

This practice is universally healing and the person doing
the forgiving is successfully bridging, or connecting to,
his/her higher mind, creating new-found hope, faith, and
trust in the ability to create healthy, loving relationships.

CHAPTER SEVEN

Reconnect To Your Spirit: *I Am*

This is the most rewarding part of the process. There is nothing you have to do. There is nothing you have to figure out. Simply let your mind be still. Now that you are no longer distracted, anxious, worried or fearful, you have opened the way to clear your mind and connect to your higher self, where you receive the characteristics or traits of higher-mind thinking. This allows you to bring these traits into your love relationships and to attract those with similar traits.

Now that you are no longer distracted and can let your mind be still, you are empowered to start engaging in some type of practice that will allow wisdom and calm, peaceful thoughts into your relationships. Let your mind receive and connect to them. Engage in activities to strengthen the connection. Meditation, prayer, nature hikes, gardening, 12-step programs, playing sports, running, engaging in the arts, reading, journaling, playing games, expressing gratitude, yoga, joining an encouragement group, dancing, and cooking are only a few options. You'll meet great people through these activities—people who are also invested in connecting this way. Develop a spirituality/peace plan, something that you will do daily, weekly, or monthly to clear your mind and allow the spiritual traits to come into your thinking.

EXERCISE 1:

List some loving qualities you want to nurture within yourself, so that you can see them mirrored in the person you attract.

_____

_____

_____

_____

_____

_____

EXERCISE 2:

Write down all the things that you wish you had the time to do and haven't been able to fit into your schedule.

_____

_____

_____

_____

_____

_____

EXERCISE 3:

Make 5 affirmations that you can repeat—one for each day of the work week. For example:

- I am going to be more tolerant and patient.
- I want to be intimate with my own feelings, so that I can be accountable for them in my relationships.
- I am grateful for the blessings I have and the love I can give.
- I will be introspective today. I will think of any upsetting situations that have occurred so far and address them with the techniques I have learned.
- Today I will nurture myself and my partner.
- This week, there have been satisfying and taxing experiences in my relationships. I have learned

some important things about myself and my partner. I will use this information to help us to grow.

- I have stayed in the present and not allowed my past to dictate what I attract into my life today.

- I have not been distracted with inappropriate behaviors. I have replaced fear with faith.

Now, write your own.

1. _____

2. _____

3. _____

4. _____

5. _____

Commit to follow through with your plan.

In summary, attracting love is a creative journey. It is our hope that by completing this workbook, you have an appreciation of how important your self-concept is in magnetizing the person you want to love. We hope this information has been helpful to you and that you will become passionate about loving and accepting yourself. You have now learned that your inner relationship is the key to attracting a loving, spiritual relationship that will fit into your life and sustain your new belief system. We wish you love.

Vicki and Ellie

The Five Steps of the Rapid Advance Process

RELINQUISHMENT of JUDGMENT	THOUGHT OF PEACE
1. **Reveal Your History**	*It happened.* It was
2. **Recognize Your Impasse**	*It is still happening.* It is.
3. **Release Your Past**	*I can forgive.* I can.
4. **Respond to Your Fear**	*I stop and look within.* I know.
5. **Reconnect to Your Spirit**	*I find myself.* I am.

ABOUT THE AUTHORS

Ellie Izzo, PhD, LPC

Ellie has been in clinical practice for over 30 years. She also serves as a trainer, Divorce Coach and Child Specialist in Collaborative Divorce cases. She developed the Rapid Advance Process, a standardized five-session brief model of counseling that was presented at the American Counseling Association convention in Atlanta in 1997 and with Vicki Carpel Miller in Honolulu in 2008. Ellie is the author of The Bridge To I Am, a self-help book outlining the Rapid Advance Process. Ellie hosted a call-in radio show in Phoenix and served as Self-Help

Editor for a nationally syndicated trade magazine. She runs several ongoing groups called the Encouragers where people meet to offer each other peace, support and acceptance.

Vicki Carpel Miller, BSN, MS, LMFT

Vicki Carpel Miller is a licensed Marriage and Family Therapist in clinical practice for over 20 years. Vicki was instrumental in bringing Collaborative Divorce to Arizona and functions as a Divorce Coach and Child Specialist in Collaborative Divorce cases. She specializes in the treatment of Vicarious Trauma, the Rapid Advance Process, the practice of Collaborative Divorce and other divorce-related issues such as blended family and stepfamily issues. Vicki is internationally recognized as a trainer with the Collaborative Divorce Training Team.

Vicki and Ellie are co-founders of the Collaborative Divorce Institute and the Vicarious Trauma Institute. Their offices are located in Scottsdale, Arizona.

Visit the author's website at:
www.vicarioustrauma.com

Contact them to speak at your next event or training:
collaborate119@aol.com
ellieizzophd@gmail.com

More books from HCI Press at unHookedBooks.com

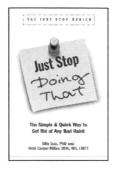

Available from unHookedBooks.com

To order, call 480-420-6355 or visit our online bookstore at unHookedBooks.com.

Visa, MasterCard, Amex
(prices subject to change without notice)

CPSIA information can be obtained at www.ICGtesting.com
Printed in the USA
BVOW011941121011

273506BV00001B/7/P

9 781936 268245